THE NATURE KIDS GUIDE TO

WOLVERINES

DAVID ANDERSON

LP Media Inc. Publishing
Text copyright © 2026 by LP Media Inc.
All rights reserved.

For information address LP Media Inc. Publishing,
30012 Variolite St NW, Princeton MN 55371
www.lpmedia.org

Publication Data

Wolverines
The Nature Kid's Guide to Wolverines — First edition.

Summary: "Learn all about Wolverines, the Nature Kid Way"
— Provided by publisher.

ISBN: 979-8-89818-139-0

[1. Wolverines - Non-Fiction] I. Title.

Title: The Nature Kid's Guide to Wolverines

CONTENTS

FROZEN FORESTS

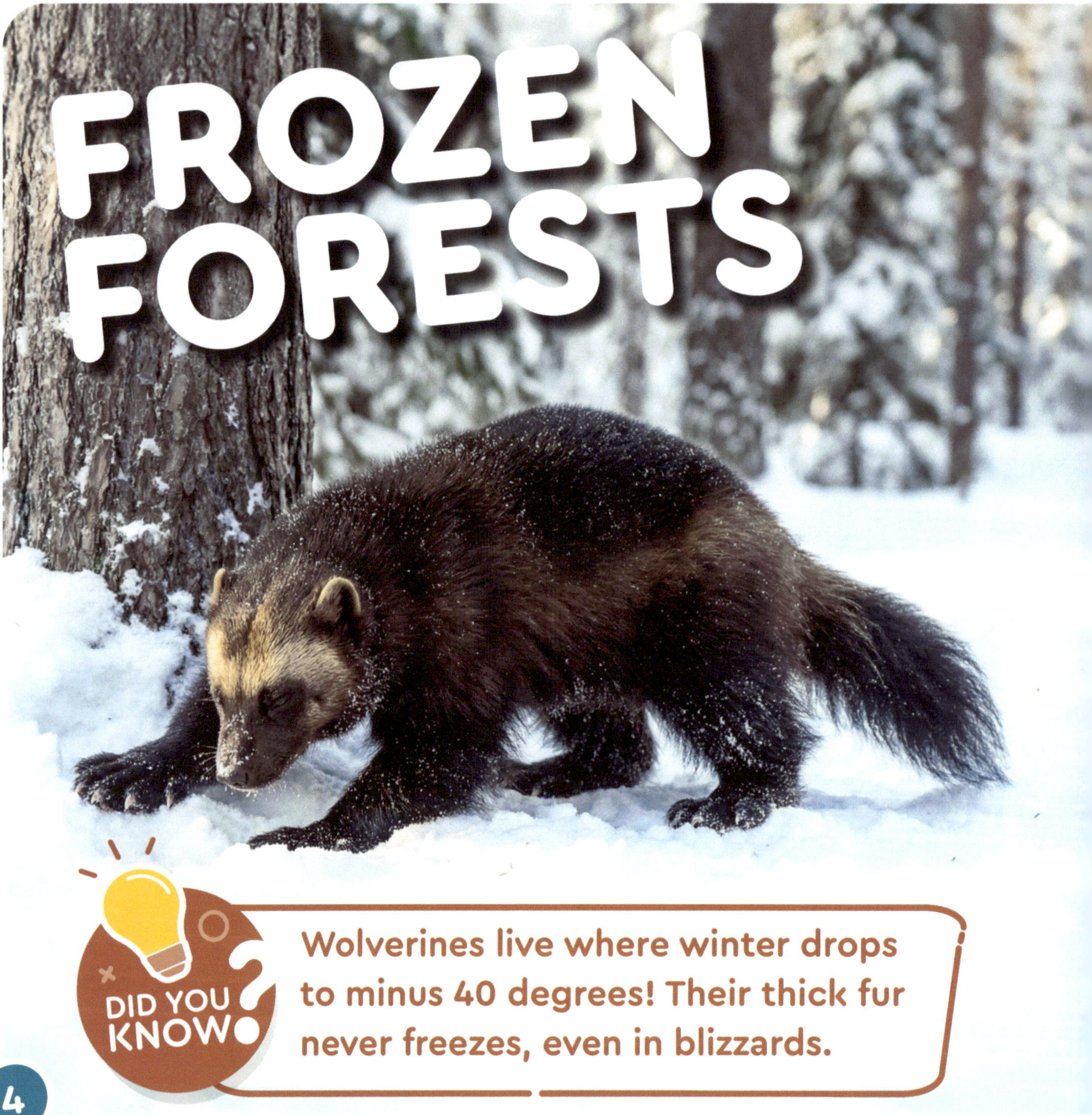

DID YOU KNOW?

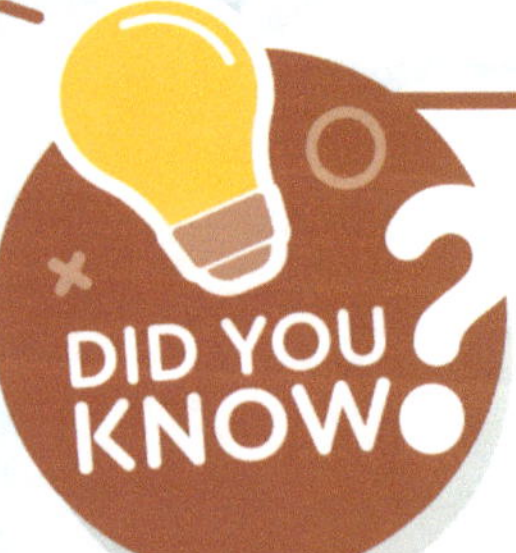

Wolverines live where winter drops to minus 40 degrees! Their thick fur never freezes, even in blizzards.

Growl! A wolverine digs through deep snow. It hunts for hidden food.

Wolverines live in cold places. They make their homes in forests and mountains where snow covers the ground for most of the year.

These tough animals live in the far north. You can find them in Alaska and Canada. Some live in Russia and northern Europe too.

A male wolverine's home range can be up to 500 square miles. They roam through thick forests, climb rocky mountains, and cross frozen lakes.

Their **habitat** stays cold and wild. Very few people live in these areas. Wolverines like it that way!

WILD TRAVELERS

Crunch! A wolverine crosses a frozen river. It keeps moving and moving.

Wolverines can travel far. They walk many miles each day. They look for food. One wolverine walked over 500 miles in just 42 days!

Their big feet work like snowshoes. This helps them walk on top of deep snow while other animals sink.

Wolverines are always on the move. Snow or sun, they never stop.

A wolverine once climbed 5,000 feet up a mountain in just 90 minutes. That is fast hiking!

SMALL BUT STRONG

Thump! A wolverine lands softly in the snow. It's chasing a meal.

Wolverines are about the size of a medium dog. They weigh between 20 to 55 pounds.

But wolverines are very strong for their size. They can drag food that weighs three times more than they do!

Wolverines are so brave they can scare off wolves and even bears. They use their strength and fierce attitude. Size does not matter to a wolverine!

Wolverines are the largest members of the weasel family on land! Only otters are bigger.

BUILT TOUGH

DID YOU KNOW?
Wolverine claws grow up to four inches long and can dig through frozen ground!

Snap! A wolverine bites through frozen bone with ease.

Wolverines have bodies made for survival. Their thick fur keeps them warm in freezing weather. The fur is oily, water and snow run off without sticking.

Their jaws are incredibly powerful. Sharp, strong teeth let wolverines crush bones that other animals cannot break.

Wolverines have large paws that work like snowshoes. Each paw has five toes with long, curved claws. These claws help them climb trees and dig through hard ice.

SUPER SNIFFERS

Sniff! A wolverine smells food buried under ten feet of snow.

Wolverines can smell food from miles away. Their powerful noses find dead animals hidden deep under the snow.

Their ears also help them hunt. They pick up small sounds in the quiet forest.

Their eyes are small and do not see very well. But wolverines do not need good eyes. Their amazing noses do most of the work!

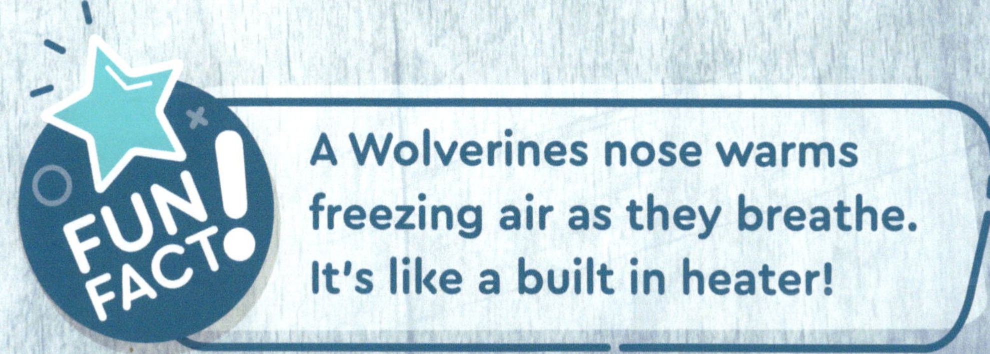

FIERCE
FIGHTERS

Snarl! A wolverine shows its teeth at a hungry wolf.

Wolverines are very fierce. They are small but brave. They will fight animals much bigger than them.

Their sharp claws and strong jaws make great weapons. They can hurt a larger **predator** with speed and fearlessness.

Wolverines spray a bad smell when scared. This stinky spray says "stay away!" Many animals avoid wolverines. They are too fierce to fight!

Wolverines are clever scavengers. They follow wolf trails to find leftover meals.

16

Chomp! A wolverine digs through snow to find a frozen meal.

Wolverines eat almost anything. They hunt rabbits and squirrels. They catch birds too. Sometimes they catch animals much bigger than themselves.

Wolverines also eat dead animals. Dead animals are called **carrion**. Wolverines find frozen bodies under the snow. Their strong jaws crunch through frozen meat.

In summer, berries fill their bellies. They eat roots too. Wolverines store extra food under rocks.

They also hide food under snow for later.

GRAB IT

Wolverines can run through snow at speeds up to 30 miles per hour to catch prey!

Pounce! A wolverine spots an injured caribou. The hunt is on!

Wolverines use surprise attacks to catch **prey**. They hide and wait for animals to pass by. Then they jump out fast!

Their strong legs help them pounce on prey. Wolverines can even take down caribou, which are five times their size! They use sharp claws to hold on tight.

Wolverines also chase prey through deep snow. Their wide paws work like snowshoes. They run on top while other animals sink. This makes catching dinner much easier for these fierce hunters.

WATCH OUT

Screech! A golden eagle spots a wolverine kit.

Wolverines have few enemies. It's too dangerous for predators to attack an adult.

Gray wolves are the main predator. A wolf pack can surround a lone wolverine. But wolverines often get away. They climb trees. They hide in rocky dens.

But young wolverines face more danger. Golden eagles hunt wolverine **kits**. They swoop down from the sky. Wolves and mountain lions attack young wolverines too.

Golden eagles can spot a wolverine kit from over a mile away.

FIGHT BACK

Hiss! A wolverine spins around to face a wolf. It will not run.

Wolverines stand their ground when threatened. They arch their backs and puff up their fur. This makes them look bigger and scarier.

Loud growls warn enemies to stay away. Their strong spray also drives off attackers.

If fighting is needed, wolverines bite and slash with sharp claws. Most predators decide to leave them alone.

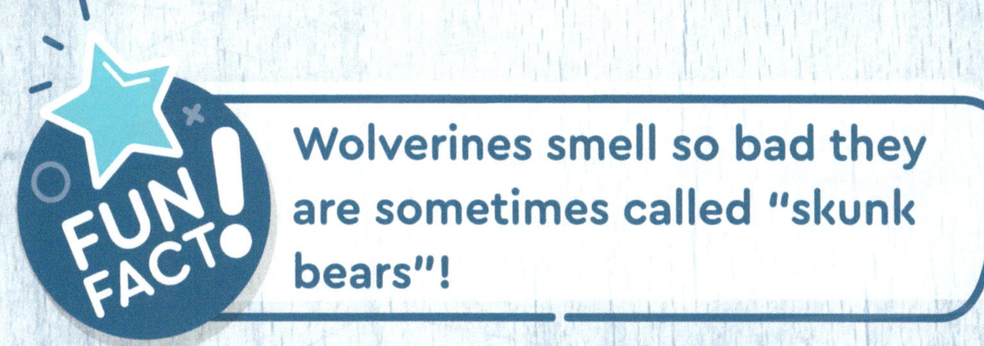

Wolverines smell so bad they are sometimes called "skunk bears"!

SNOW STOMPERS

Stomp! A wolverine walks across soft snow. Its big paws do not sink.

Wolverines travel long distances every day. They walk about 15 miles searching for food.

Their wide paws spread their weight on snow. Each paw is as big as a human hand! This helps them move fast over soft ground without sinking down.

Wolverines also climb can climb up steep mountains. Strong legs carry them over rocks and ice.

Wolverine paws have rough pads that grip ice. They walk on snow other animals fall through.

DAY AND
NIGHT

Rustle! A wolverine wakes up in its den. Night falls outside.

Wolverines are active at any hour. They do not follow a set schedule.

These tough animals hunt during the day. They also look for food at night. Wolverines only rest when they feel tired.

In winter, wolverines are active during the day. In summer, they like cool morning hours. Their strong sense of smell helps them find food anytime.

Wolverines stay active for 3 to 4 hours at a time. Then they rest and start again!

LONE WOLVES

Crack! A wolverine walks on a frozen log. It is alone. No pack follows.

Wolverines live alone most of the year. They do not form packs like wolves do.

Each wolverine has its own land. Males roam up to 500 square miles! Females stay in smaller areas.

Adult wolverines only meet to mate. Then they go off on there own again until the next year.

A male wolverine's land may overlap with two or three female territories nearby.

A male wolverine sniffs the air. He follows a scent trail. A female is close by.

Wolverines mate in late spring and summer. Males and females find each other by smell.

A male wolverine may travel hundreds of miles. He wants to find a female. He crosses mountains and valleys. His strong nose shows him the way.

Wolverine mothers can put their babies "on pause." The tiny egg waits inside the mother for months. It only starts growing when the mother is healthy and has plenty of food.

TINY KITS

Wolverine mothers usually have two or three kits at a time. Some litters have four! Kits are born blind.

Squeak! Tiny wolverine kits tumble in their snow den.

Wolverine babies are called kits. They are born in late winter inside a cozy snow den.

Newborn kits weigh less than one pound. They have soft white fur. Their eyes stay closed for about three weeks.

Kits grow fast on their mother's milk. By summer, they follow her outside. Young wolverines stay with their mother for up to two years.

Kits learn to hunt by watching their mother. She teaches them to find food under snow.

Sometimes wolverine dads help too! When kits are big enough, their father may teach them where to find food.

MIGHTY MOMS

Mother wolverines can drag prey that weighs more than they do!

Grunt! A mother wolverine carries food to her den, where hungry kits wait.

Mother wolverines work hard to raise their young. They build warm dens deep in the snow.

Mothers nurse their kits for about ten weeks. They also bring meat back to the den for growing babies. By spring, kits are ready to eat solid food.

Mothers teach kits everything they need to survive. Young wolverines learn to climb, dig, and find prey.

A mother protects her kits fiercely. She moves them to a new den if she senses danger.

WARMING
WORLD

Whoosh! Warm winds blow across the mountains. The heat makes snow melt fast.

Wolverines need cold places to live. But climate change is making their home warmer.

Snow dens keep baby wolverines safe and warm. When snow melts too early, mothers cannot protect their kits.

Warming also spoils the food wolverines store in snowbanks. Animals they eat may move to cooler areas.

Scientists put special collars on wolverines to track them. This shows where they travel as the climate warms up.

HELPING
HANDS

Click! A scientist puts a tracking collar on a wolverine.

People help wolverines. Scientists track them. They learn where wolverines go.

Countries protect land for wolverines. These safe areas give them room to roam. Wolverines can raise their kits there.

People build wildlife crossings too. These bridges help wolverines cross busy roads safely.

In Montana, special cameras take photos of wild wolverines. This helps scientists count them!

GLOSSARY

habitat
The place where an animal lives and finds food.

carrion
Dead animals that other animals eat for food.

predator
An animal that hunts and eats other animals.

prey
An animal that gets hunted and eaten by other animals.

kits
Baby wolverines.